SILVER BURDETT PROFESSIONAL PUBLICATIONS

Classroom Teacher Series

Handicapped People in Society:
Ideas and Activities for Teachers

Hints for Teaching Social Studies

Improving Behavior:
100 Applications for the Elementary Classroom

Mathematics Games for Classroom Use

The Preschool Framework:
A Planning Method with Activities

Hints for

SILVER BURDETT PROFESSIONAL PUBLICATIONS

CLASSROOM TEACHERS

Joan Marie Brown

SILVER BURDETT COMPANY
Morristown, New Jersey
Glenview, Illinois • **Palo Alto** • **Dallas** • **Atlanta**

Cover Victoria Beller-Smith for Silver Burdett.

HINTS FOR CLASSROOM TEACHERS

© 1980 SILVER BURDETT COMPANY.

All rights reserved.

Printed in the United States of America

Published simultaneously in Canada

ISBN 0-382-02694-2

Library of Congress Card Number: 79-65626

PREFACE

Many students would describe a good teacher
as one who likes children,
is well-prepared, consistent, and fair.
However, as most teachers know,
one does not become a "good teacher" overnight.
Teaching is a learning process—
one that requires time, patience, and experience.

This book is designed to assist you
in reaching those goals.
It is based on much teaching experience,
many successes and failures,
and numerous conversations with colleagues.
It is filled with hints
to assist you in the classroom.

I wish to thank my husband,
mother-in-law, and friends
for their support and interest
throughout this project.
I also wish to acknowledge Barbara Glispin
for her secretarial assistance, and Eleanor Fisher,
Mary Christensen, and Ruth Glispin
for their critical reading of the manuscript.

Finally, I dedicate this guide
to you, the teacher,
with the hope that it may help you
with your students and your teaching.

Joan Marie Brown

CONTENTS

Prologue

W HAT IS A GOOD TEACHER? THESE ARE SOME OF THE responses made by eighth- and ninth-grade students to my question, "How would you describe a good teacher?"

"A fair teacher is a good teacher; one who doesn't show favoritism. I like a teacher who has a sense of humor and who jokes around once in a while at the right time. I like a teacher who isn't super strict but just strict enough. I don't like teachers who grade real tough, but just hard enough so you'll work hard."

"Good teachers know what they are talking about and are willing to listen to the opinions of their students."

"A good teacher makes work interesting and gives the students a break once in a while."

"What I expect out of a teacher is control over students, because you have to have that before you can do anything."

"I also expect a teacher to help me without embarrassing me, so I won't feel dumb when asking questions."

"I like teachers with a sense of humor, because I think it is easier on the kids and on themselves; everyone is more relaxed."

"I expect a teacher to be friendly and fair to all students. There are some students who are really slow, and there are some teachers who are so rude that they make fun of these kids in front of the class. I don't expect this from a teacher."

"I think that a teacher should be patient. If someone doesn't understand something, the teacher should keep explaining until that person understands; that's what teachers are paid for—to teach!"

"A good teacher

- makes the class interesting
- has variety
- doesn't have a closed mind
- doesn't pick favorites
- is interested in the subject being taught
- can joke around
- can control the class
- doesn't get hyper all the time."

"I think that teachers should have certain rules they enforce to keep the room in order, but I don't think it should be like a prison cell. Then again, it shouldn't be chaos either!"

"A good teacher to me is a teacher who doesn't yell a lot, who will find out what the problem is without jumping to conclusions, and who treats the students with respect."

"A good teacher is one who doesn't yell all the time, teaches things clearly, gives some free time, and gets along well with kids."

"A good teacher
- can control a class with a minimum amount of yelling and detentions
- can communicate with and understand the pupils
- should also be sort of exciting and fun to be around
- can teach you information without dragging it out
- is a person, not a machine!"

"A good teacher
- can lead a discussion
- listens to students
- has a good sense of humor
- should know more than just the technical aspects of the subject
- should go at the pace of the class
- shouldn't put students down."

"A good teacher
- knows the subject
- accepts slower-learning kids and helps them more
- is just as nice to unpopular kids as to popular ones
- is nice but still in control
- treats the kids as individuals."

"I think a good teacher
- is nice to the students but has discipline
- makes the class as interesting as possible
- has authority but does not overuse it."

1

The Teacher and the Classroom

THE CLASSROOM IS THE PHYSICAL ENVIRONMENT IN which learning takes place. This environment includes chalkboards, bulletin boards, bookcases, desks, and chairs. The maintenance and the management of these variables should be effectively and efficiently controlled by the classroom teacher so that a productive learning situation results.

Classroom Maintenance

A pleasant, safe, comfortable classroom is important because it encourages learning and good behavior. It is wise to consider the following questions when attempting to keep a classroom in good condition.

- Is the room comfortable? Is it too hot? Is it too cold? Do the lights work? Does a window need to be opened or closed?

- Is the room safe? Are any of the windows broken or cracked? Are the maps and the movie screen securely fastened? Are any of the chairs or desks broken? Do the electrical outlets work?

- Can you hear the fire-drill alarm from your room? Do you know how to exit in case of an emergency?

- Is the room neat and clean?

- Does each student have adequate work space?

- Do the locks on your door work?

- Does the pencil sharpener work?

If any of the equipment mentioned above is not working properly, it becomes your responsibility to notify your principal and a custodian, *in writing,* about the problem. If you do not do so and an accident occurs, you become liable. Remember, it is your professional responsibility to provide a safe environment for your students.

The Bulletin Board

A bulletin board serves several purposes, and if it is used wisely, it becomes a place for academic as well as student-centered information. If you want a successful bulletin board, here are some points to consider:

- It should be colorful and simple so that it draws attention and can be read quickly and understood easily.
- It should display materials that have something to do with the subject being taught, such as students' work, maps, posters, charts, newspaper articles, and letters.
- It should be fun. Comics, holiday decorations, students' poems or drawings, and famous sayings are all things that could be displayed in a fun corner.
- It should be a source of information. It is also an excellent place to display school bulletins, lunch menus, sports schedules, and the bus list.
- It should be changed frequently to add variety to the classroom.

A well-displayed bulletin board tells students that you care about your room and that you want it to look attractive for them. However, if you are not talented in this area enlist the aid of some of your interested, talented students and have them construct a bulletin board display for you.

Sample Bulletin Board Layout

EDUCATIONAL MATERIAL	*FUN CORNER*
Maps, current events, pictures, articles, samples of documents, charts, graphs, headlines, illustrations, and so forth.	Comics, students' work, holiday decorations, famous sayings, and so forth.
	INFORMATION
	Menus, sports schedules, bus schedules, school calendar, and so forth.

The Chalkboard

The chalkboard is an important part of the classroom. All types of information can be conveyed by properly using this means of communication. Here are a few hints you may wish to consider when using this teaching tool:

1. Always write clearly on the chalkboard so that students seated in the back of the room can read it.
2. Keep the chalkboard clean so that it will be easy to read.
3. Make sure there is no reflection on the chalkboard. If necessary, draw the shades.
4. Use a small piece of chalk. Large pieces have a tendency to squeak.
5. Don't stand or sit directly in front of the chalkboard, particularly when students need to see it.
6. Don't write too far down on the chalkboard or students will have a difficult time reading it.
7. The chalkboard can be used to record
   - the date
   - daily assignments
   - reminders
   - summaries
   - maps, charts, pictures
   - vocabulary words
   - questions
   - lesson formats
   - famous sayings
   - joke or thought for the day.
8. Write "Please Save" next to the material you wish to save for a day or more so that the custodian will not erase it.

Sample Chalkboard

DATE: 4/7/80

PLEASE SAVE

THOUGHT FOR THE DAY
Smiles are contagious!

REMINDERS:
1st and 4th periods, test on Immigration Unit—04/14

2nd period students,
permission slips for
field trip must be in by
4/12

ASSIGNMENT

2nd, 3rd, 6th periods
1. View film—*How to Interview*
2. Please answer the following questions using complete sentences.

A. Whom would you have hired and why?
B. Whom would you have *not* hired and why?
C. List five questions the interviewer asked each applicant.

Desks

Desks that can be moved offer a great deal of flexibility for the teacher. Desks can be arranged in rows for individual work, moved together for groupwork, placed in a circle for round-table discussions, or turned so that students face each other for panel discussions or class meetings. The options are many, and movable desks give a teacher opportunities to plan a wide range of activities.

Shelves and Bookcases

Fill your shelves and bookcases with magazines, puzzles, reference materials, and a file of extra credit assignments. Properly filed materials can be located readily, making it easier for both students and teacher to use them. Students will appreciate this area of the classroom because they will be able to find constructive activities to occupy their free time.

Classroom Charts

By making and displaying a chart like the one suggested below, a teacher is better able to keep accurate count of all the classroom materials that have been loaned out to students.

Sign Out Chart

ITEMS ON LOAN

Date	Name	Period	Item	Date Returned
1/8	Joan Glispin	2nd	ditto "Am I a Wise Consumer?"	1/7
1/10	Michael Brown	1st	book *Prejudice: The Invisible Wall*	1/11
2/7	Mary Berry	6th	globe	2/9

Assignment Charts

By maintaining charts like the ones illustrated, a teacher can better remember which assignments he or she assigned on a particular day to each individual period. These charts also aid those students who were absent as they know by a glance which materials and what assignment directions to request.

FIRST PERIOD	AMERICAN MINORITIES
1/9	Essay, 150 words, What is an individual?
1/11	Read ditto "Boy in the Ghetto." Do all the questions at the end of the story.
1/12	List ten ways a person can handle prejudice.

SECOND PERIOD	CONSUMER AND CAREER EXPLORATION
1/10	Read ditto "Bargains." Do all the questions at the end of the article.
1/12	Essay Questions 75 words each A. Define impulse buying. Give an example. B. Define planned purchase. Give an example. C. Complete the following sentence: To me, financial security is . . .
1/15	Complete ditto "Your Consumer Profile."

2

The Teacher
and the Curriculum

A TEACHER DEALS WITH THE IMPLEMENTATION OF curriculum every day when arranging for field trips and guest speakers, preparing lesson plans, assigning homework, leading discussions, writing tests, or grading papers. This is a major part of teaching and each teacher handles curriculum decisions in individual ways. In this section, you will find a variety of suggested methods for managing this particular aspect of teaching.

Lesson Plans

Lesson plans are important. Through careful planning, lessons become organized, prepared, and structured. Careful planning also produces a permanent collection of successful teaching ideas.

This section provides a model lesson plan that includes directions for formulating your own lesson plans. Teachers should select those parts of this format that are relevant to their own personality and teaching needs.

This section also contains four sample lesson plans that were written for four different units, as well as directions on how to evaluate a lesson plan.

The model format presented below can be used as a guide when creating or recording daily lesson plans for any unit of study.

DAILY LESSON PLAN FORMAT

Aims

State the skill, the attitude, or the concept you wish your students to develop through this lesson.

Methodology

State how you are going to accomplish the aims of this lesson. What are you going to do? What are you going to have your students do?

Materials

List the resources you will use to implement this lesson (textbook, filmstrip, equipment, reference materials, and so forth).

Evaluation

Evaluate the lesson. Ask yourself questions such as, What was good about it? What parts of it should be kept? What parts should be deleted?

Suggestions

Write down any ideas that occur to you for improvising the lesson. State how the lesson could be extended, or note that students needed more time for the assignment.

This lesson plan was written for an American Minorities class. It is a model of a plan for a pamphlet lesson.

SAMPLE LESSON PLAN—PAMPHLET

Unit Title: The Changing Role of Men, Women, and Children Within American Society

Lesson Title: Men and Women in Different Cultures (two periods)

Aims

1. That students be able to identify Arapesh, Mundugumor, and American cultures.

2. That students be able to identify and analyze similarities among these three cultures.

3. That students be able to identify and analyze the differences among these cultural styles.

Methodology

1. Review yesterday's lesson by asking students to describe nineteenth- and twentieth-century men and women.

2. Distribute the American Education Press (A.E.P.) booklet, *The American Woman.* Ask students to open their booklets to page 33, Chapter Four, "The Male and Female in Other Societies."

3. Introduce Chapter Four with these two questions:
   - What does feminine mean to you?
   - What does masculine mean to you?

4. Read aloud and discuss Chapter Four with students.

5. Hand out copies of the chart shown below and ask students to work in groups of two to complete the chart.

COMPARING SOCIETIES			
	Arapesh	**Mundugumor**	**American**
What is considered manly?			
What is considered womanly?			
How is a boy child raised?			
How is a girl child raised?			

6. Ask students to save their papers so they can be discussed the next day.

7. Next day, place the chart form on the chalkboard and fill it in as a class.

8. When the chart discussion is completed ask the students to consider the following questions: Which society do you find most appealing? Why? Discuss these questions as a class. Collect the students' papers and grade them.

Materials

1. A.E.P. Booklet, *The American Woman*
2. Handout—chart
3. Chalkboard

Evaluation

1. Discussion went well because students were given a chance to consider the new information before they discussed it.

2. Students were very interested in the Arapesh and Mundugumor cultures.

Suggestions

A panel discussion could be set up using the following questions: Which society do you find most appealing? Why?

The following lesson illustrates how to develop a chapter review lesson.

SAMPLE LESSON PLAN—TEXTBOOK

Course: American History

Lesson: The Thirteen Colonies (one period)

Aims

1. To give students a review of Chapter Four.
2. To develop the skill of following directions.

Methodology

1. Distribute charts like the one shown and explain the directions to students.

2. Tell students they will use *European Colonies in America,* Chapter Four, pp. 65-82, for this assignment.

3. Tell students they may work in groups of two to do this assignment.

4. Tell students their papers are due at the end of the period.

5. Permit students to form their own groups before beginning work on this assignment.

		THE ORIGINAL THIRTEEN COLONIES		
Name	*First Permanent Settlement*	*Date*	*Founder*	*Reason for Founding*
1.				
2.				
3.				
4.				
5.				
6.				
7.				
8.				
9.				
10.				
11.				
12.				
13.				

Materials

1. Chart handouts
2. U.S. History textbook

Evaluation

Good review assignment. Students enjoyed the groupwork and the chart format.

Suggestions

Extend the amount of time to one and one-half periods when repeating this assignment.

This lesson plan was written for the day of a test in a Consumer Education class.

SAMPLE LESSON PLAN—TEST

Course: Consumer Education

Lesson: Consumer Test—Unit One (one period)

Aim

To determine if students have grasped the basic consumer knowledge taught in this unit.

Methodology

1. Distribute copies of the test shown. Read each question aloud to see if students understand the test questions.

TEST

Unit One—Are You a Wise Consumer?
Directions: Answer each question using complete sentences.
Each question is worth 10 points.

1. Who is a consumer?
2. What is a small-claims court?
3. What is the purpose of the Better Business Bureau?
4. How does a warranty help the consumer?
5. How do labels help the consumer?
6. List two consumer rights.
7. List two consumer responsibilities.
8. How does *Consumer Reports* help the consumer?
9. What is comparison shopping?
10. List five things that will help make a person a wise consumer.

2. Require complete silence during the test.
3. Tell students they may work on a crossword puzzle or read a magazine after they have completed the test.

Materials

Test handout

Evaluations

Fair test. Almost all students passed with a C or better!

Suggestions

Change test questions as follows:

4. What is a warranty? How does a warranty help the consumer?

9. Define comparison shopping.   Give an example of comparison shopping.

This next plan demonstrates how to write a lesson when using a film as the instructional medium.   This plan was used in a Career Education class.

SAMPLE LESSON PLAN—FILM

Course: Career Education

Unit: Interviewing

Lesson: *How to Interview*—film (one period)

Aim

To show students the correct procedure for job interviews.

Methodology

1. Give students the following information about the film:

    a. Three girls are interviewed for the same job.

b. Susan is interviewed first, Toni second, and Dolores last.

c. These girls do not know that they are being filmed during their interviews.

2. Tell students they will be responsible for answering the following questions when the film is finished. Write the questions on the chalkboard.

    a. What did Susan do correctly during her interview? What could she have done differently?

    b. What did Toni do correctly during her interview? What could she have done differently?

    c. What did Dolores do correctly during her interview? What could she have done differently?

    d. Which girl would you have hired?

    e. What four questions did the interviewer ask each girl?

3. Show the film *How to Interview* (18 minutes).

4. Have students either write out the answers to the questions in item 2 or participate in a class discussion.

Materials

1. Film projector
2. Film: *How to Interview*
3. Paper and pencil

Evaluation

Excellent film. Students learned what to do and what not to do by observing these three interviews.

Suggestion

This lesson could be extended for two more days. Students could prepare and then perform simulated job interviews in front of the class.

The following lesson was written for a class in Government. It illustrates how to develop a plan using teacher made materials.

SAMPLE LESSON PLAN—TEACHER DEVELOPED MATERIALS

Unit Title: Congress

Lesson Title: How to Write a Letter to a Legislator (two periods)

Aims

1. To make students aware that citizens can make their concerns known by writing to their Senators and Representatives in Congress.
2. To show students how to compose a formal letter.

Methodology

1. Discuss the following two questions with students. Have a student list all the answers on the chalkboard.
   a. What are some of America's greatest concerns?
   b. What are some of America's greatest problems?
2. Read the list back to the class when students have finished responding. Then ask students to provide solutions.
3. Pass out a sample letter to a member of Congress. Read it aloud and discuss with students how it is constructed.
4. When writing a letter to a legislator:
   - Always be respectful.
   - Make your point quickly.
   - Be precise.
   - Ask questions if you wish.
   - Ask for information if you wish.
   - Be neat.
   - Write clearly.
   - Spell all words correctly.
   - Follow an accepted letter format.
5. Now let students choose an issue and have them write a letter to a representative in Congress. Have addresses available for students.

127 Curtis
Dearborn, MI 48127
March 31, 1969

Senator Philip A. Hart
Senate Office Building
Washington, DC 20510

Dear Senator:
Keep up the good work on limiting the ABM, probing the auto manufacturers, and not conforming to the status-quo. In my opinion, you will be unbeatable in 1970!

Sincerely,

Ronald G. Brown

6. As students finish, check and grade their letters pointing out spelling and grammar errors. When this is done, have students recopy their letters.
7. Have students address an envelope, enclose the letter, stamp it and mail it.

Materials

1. Sample letter—ditto

2. Chalkboard

3. Paper, envelopes, and stamps

Evaluation

Excellent. Students were very excited that their letters would actually be mailed and answered.

Suggestion

Make a bulletin board with the responses from the government officials.

HOW TO EVALUATE A LESSON PLAN

It is always wise to evaluate a lesson plan. It is especially important if the lesson plan fell short of your expectations the first time around. Effective evaluation can be accomplished by considering the following questions.

- Were my aims relevant and realistic?
- Was I enthusiastic?
- Was I well prepared?
- Was my presentation organized and clear?
- Was my presentation varied enough?
- Did my students understand what they were doing and why they were doing it?
- Were my directions clear and to the point?
- Were my questions well phrased in language the students could understand?
- Did the students respond properly to my questions?
- How many resources did I use?
- Did I find time to talk to each student individually?
- Did I enjoy working with my students today?
- Did all the students listen to and take part in today's lesson?

Homework

Homework can be an important part of the student's process of learning. It can be an extension of a day's lesson, preparation for a new lesson, or the culminating activity for a unit of study. Homework assignments should be well thought out and relevant to the subject matter being taught. Here are some suggestions on this particular aspect of teaching:

1. Place the homework assignment on the chalkboard indicating the date it is due. Students can then copy down this information and refer to it when needed.
2. Give the homework assignment during class when there is adequate time for explanation and student questions.
3. Don't always give the same kind of assignment (example: "Do the questions at the end of the chapter."). Vary your assignments.
4. When possible use the previous day's homework as the basis for a class discussion, for review purposes, or as a lead-in for the new lesson you are presenting.
5. Homework assignments should be realistic. Do students have enough knowledge to do the work assigned? Will they have the materials needed at home to successfully complete the work? How long should it take to do the assignment?
6. Always collect the student's work the day it is due.
7. Grade the homework papers and return them to the students as soon as possible.
8. Notify parents if a student continually fails to do the assigned homework. Parents have a right to know if their son or daughter is not doing the assigned work.

Audiovisual Materials

Audiovisual (AV) materials are an important part of the modern classroom. If the material is selected carefully it can add a new and creative dimension to your teaching. AV material can be used effectively to

- Motivate students
- Introduce a unit
- Review a unit
- Illustrate a new concept
- Dramatize a point
- Encourage a discussion
- Summarize a lesson
- Add variety to a teaching situation

- Cover a large amount of material in a short span of time
- Reinforce curriculum previously taught
- Aid students who learn aurally

For successful results, when using audiovisual materials, you should know how to properly operate the following audiovisual equipment.

- movie projector
- slide projector
- overhead projector
- opaque projector
- film-loop projector
- filmstrip projector
- tape recorder
- videotape machine
- record player
- copy machine
- mimeograph machine
- thermofax machine

In your particular teaching situation you may find it necessary to learn how to use other, more sophisticated equipment as well.

Questions

Questions can be used effectively for written assignments, for tests, and for directing discussions. Questions must be well formulated if students are expected to think and respond to them intelligently. Formulating good questions takes time and forethought. A teacher must decide what types of answers are required: fact or opinion, comparison or contrast, outline or summary, definition or explanation. The next several pages offer a listing of the types of questions that might be used, as well as suggestions on how to lead a discussion.

To stimulate a good discussion or an effective written assignment, you must ask thought-provoking questions. Some examples of such questions are provided below.

SAMPLE QUESTIONS

General Questions

What were the major causes of the Civil War?
What were some of the results of World War I?

Student Reaction Questions

If you were an American Indian today, how would you feel about your circumstances?
If people hated and mistreated you simply because you had blond hair, how would you handle the situation?

Thought-Provoking Questions

Why is it so important to study history?
What could have happened during World War II if the United States had not entered the war?

Cause-and-Effect Questions

What connection is there between the Boston Tea Party and the Revolutionary War?
Why did the Civil War occur?

Personalized Questions

Where would you rather live—on the frontier in 1776 or in a city in 1979? Explain your choice.
Do you think life was easier, or more difficult, for frontier women than for women of today? Explain your answer.

Descriptive Questions

Describe what life was like for a Vietnamese peasant in the early 1970s.
Tell what life was like for a New England farmer in 1865.

Compare-and-Contrast Questions

How were the North and South alike and different in 1860?
Compare and contrast the nineteenth-century woman with the twentieth-century woman.

Open-Ended Questions

What is pollution?
Keep asking the same question over and over again until there aren't any more answers. As students answer, list their responses on the chalkboard. Then have students attempt to group their answers under major titles. What you end up with is an inclusive listing and a detailed outline.

Summary Questions

Give as many examples as you can of the check and balance system.
Give an example of prejudice, stereotyping, and scapegoating.

Observation Questions

What seems to be occurring in this picture?
How does the title of this film reflect the information presented by the film?

The following suggestions should be considered when either writing or asking questions.

• Focus on only one idea when asking a question. Don't confuse your students.

- Make sure your questions are complete, or you will get just a yes or a no answer.
- Make sure your questions are clear. Could you answer them?
- In your questions use vocabulary that your students understand.
- Be sure students use complete sentences to answer questions.

Discussions

One of the keys to effective teaching is offering students the chance to share and to expand their knowledge, their ideas, and their experiences with you and with other students. Class discussions, properly managed, provide an excellent opportunity for the academic growth of your students. Listed below are some specific uses of class discussion.

- To preview material with students before a test
- To ascertain whether main concepts have been grasped by students
- To add variety to a teaching situation
- To encourage the skill of verbal communication
- To reemphasize important points
- To give students a chance to share their thoughts and knowledge
- To give students and teacher a chance to interact
- To offer the auditory and verbal learner opportunity to excel

When a discussion is correctly led, all students have an equal opportunity to become involved in the activity. It requires practice on the part of both teacher and students to master this skill. Shown below is a set of guidelines that you and your students should be aware of prior to any class discussion. If a teacher explains these guidelines to the students and consistently enforces them throughout the discussion period, an orderly discussion will result.

1. Require silence so that you can be heard and your students can hear each other.
2. Permit only one student to talk at a time so that he or she can be heard.

3. Have students raise their hands to be called on so that the discussion remains orderly.

4. Call on students when their hands are raised. Be consistent. Do not allow a shouting student to take control.

5. Let your students do the talking. Interrupt only when there is an argument brewing. Lead the discussion, don't control it.

6. Let the students know that no one person's opinion is perfect and that the purpose of a discussion is to share ideas with each other.

7. Do not interrupt a student who is talking. Let the student finish before calling on another student or commenting on what was said.

8. As a teacher, know where you want your questions to lead, and prepare them accordingly.

9. To encourage student participation during a discussion, give the seating chart to a student and have him or her award one point to each student who contributes to the discussion. Three points can equal an *A* in participation.

Tests

Included in this section are samples of an objective test and an essay test. Illustrated within these two tests are the various types of questions a teacher may use when writing and developing a test.

Tests are a means of evaluation. If tests are correctly formulated, they offer a means by which student growth can be fairly evaluated. Some possible uses of tests are identified below.

1. A pre-test/post-test method can be used for evaluating student progress.

2. Tests encourage students to review the material that was taught within a unit of study.

3. Tests show a teacher whether the students have grasped the major concepts of a unit of study.

4. Tests show whether the teacher is getting the material across to the majority of the students.

5. Tests provide a degree of objectivity in arriving at a student's overall grade.

These are only some of the functions of testing; they are not all-encompassing! In your teaching situation you may come across numerous other circumstances requiring formal testing.

In writing objective tests teachers may use any one or a combination of the following formats.

- fill-in-the-blank questions
- matching questions
- true or false questions
- short-answer questions
- multiple choice questions

This type of test is valid for determining whether a student understands the material that has been presented. Usually only one answer is correct for each question. Sample questions are given below.

SAMPLE OBJECTIVE TEST

Economics Final

Fill in the Blanks: Please use words from the list provided to complete these sentences. Some of the words may be used more than once, while others may not be used at all. (2 points each)

1. What will happen to the price of eggs if the supply of eggs is cut in half? The price will _____.

2. A _____ is something of value that can be seen or touched.

3. A _____ is something of value that cannot be seen or touched.

4. What will happen to the price of rubies if they can be made in your own kitchen? The price will _____.

5. _____, 6. _____, and

7. _____ are used to create goods and services.

8. When the demand for a good or service decreases, the _____ will also decrease.

9. _____ is the study of how people try to get the most out of their limited resources.

10. When the demand for a good or service increases, so will _____.

11. What would happen to the demand for shoelaces if they cost five times as much as they do now? The demand would _____.

12. What would happen to the demand for blue jeans if the price were greatly reduced? The demand would _____.

13. What would happen to the price of lettuce if it were in short supply? The price would _____.

14. _____ is one of the factors of production.

15. _____ is an economic system in which the government owns and operates almost all the means of production.

firm	natural resources	decrease
budget	investment	capital resources
economics	capitalism	increase
good	price	communism
service	human resources	
land	capital	

Matching: Write a letter from column B on the appropriate blank in column A. (3 points each)

A		**B**
_____1. free enterprise	a.	the right of the government to take private property for public use
_____2. competition	b.	the U.S. economic system
_____3. eminent domain	c.	the effort to outperform other businesses
_____4. capitalism	d.	the right of an individual to operate a legal business
_____5. corporation	e.	a form of business organization

True or False: Mark *T* or *F* in the space provided before each sentence. (3 points each)

_____ 1. Individuals may start any legal business in a capitalistic society.

_____ 2. Individuals may start any legal business in a socialistic society as long as it does not compete with a government business.

_____ 3. Economics is the study of the development of man.

_____ 4. A want is something a person must have to exist.

_____ 5. Profit is the main reason behind businesses in a capitalistic society.

_____ 6. A proprietorship is one of three forms of business organizations in Russia.

_____ 7. A stockbroker is a person who invests in a corporation.

_____ 8. The labor unions were developed as a result of the Industrial Revolution.

_____ 9. A monopoly encourages competition.

_____10. Income tax is one of our federal government's chief sources of money.

Short Answers: Fill in the blanks with appropriate words. (3 points each)

1. The three major economics systems are _____, _____, and _____.

2. The three major goals of a labor union are_____ _____, and _____.

3. _____, _____, and _____ are three of the four factors of production.

4. The three forms of business are _____, _____, and _____.

5. The Industrial Revolution changed the working habits of the American people by

    a. _____

    b. _____

    c. _____

Multiple Choice: Please circle the correct answer. (2 points each)

1. An example of a good is

    a. a teacher

    b. a tree

    c. an automobile

2. An example of a natural resource is

    a. oil

    b. a building

    c. a factory worker

3. Competition is an economic factor found in a

    a. capitalist economy

    b. socialist economy

    c. communist economy

4. The four factors of production are

    a. land, capital, labor, competition

    b. labor, land, management, free enterprise

    c. land, capital, management, labor

5. Which is owned by the stockholders?

    a. a proprietorship

    b. a corporation

    c. a partnership

Subjective test questions can have a variety of answers. Students show exactly what they know and understand when answering an essay question. There are two drawbacks to this type of test. It is time consuming for the teacher to correct, and it is difficult to be objective when grading this kind of test. However, if you list the main ideas that should be included in each answer, you will have a common standard to apply to all test responses. Each response then can be objectively evaluated against your list.

SAMPLE SUBJECTIVE TEST

Consumer Education Final

Please answer the following questions using complete sentences. Be sure to answer each question in detail and to include as many points of information as possible. Each answer is worth 10 points.

1. Who is a consumer?
2. Name two consumer rights.
3. Name two consumer responsibilities.
4. Please explain the following statement: Every time a consumer purchases anything, he casts his vote.
5. What is an impulse purchase? Please give an example.
6. Define comparison shopping. Please give an example.
7. When is a bargain, a bargain?
8. Give two reasons why a budget is important.
9. How does advertising affect the average consumer? Give two examples.
10. Name two agencies a consumer can turn to for help. Describe the purpose of each agency.

Grades

Decisions about grades should be based on a predetermined set of criteria. Students should be informed about the specific points that will be taken into consideration when any type of assignment is graded. This will help students know exactly what is expected from them. Besides formats for grading daily assignments and major projects, a list of criteria for final evaluation is also included in this section.

Listed below are some general guidelines that every teacher should consider when attempting to grade a student.

• Make sure you understand your school system's grading policy. How does your system define an *A*, and how are students marked on classroom behavior?

- Be prepared to explain to your students why you gave the grade you did. Explain your grading procedure for the semester, for daily assignments, for research projects, and for tests.
- Grade each student as an individual. Consider work, effort, and ability. Never penalize the students who struggle through every assignment with a low grade.
- Notify parents if a student is not passing your course. Ask for their help and cooperation. Parents deserve to know if their children are not passing.
- Make sure your objectives and your system of evaluation are not too rigid. Could you have passed your tests if you were in the student's place?
- The bell-curve does not always ring true. It really could happen that all your students do deserve *A*'s and *B*'s. It could also happen that your test was not well written, if only three students passed it.
- Don't discriminate. Do not give a student a lower academic grade simply because you do not like the student or because of a discipline problem.
- Be consistent in your grading. Do you give letter or percentage grades? Are all tests equal in importance?
- Make sure your students know at all times where they stand academically. Grade papers and tests at once and return them promptly.

Inform students at the beginning of each semester about the method you use for grading daily assignments so that they know exactly what is expected of them. Papers can be graded in several ways. Here are some criteria and a method for grading daily work.

1. Various ways to grade papers:

- You can use a check mark to indicate satisfactory, acceptable papers and a zero to indicate unsatisfactory, unacceptable papers.
- You can use letter grades

  A for exceptional   *D* for below average

  B for good   *E* or *F* for unacceptable

  C for fair

2. The following are items to consider when grading a daily assignment

- Accuracy in following directions
- Content
- Grammar
- Spelling
- Student's abilities
- Completed on time
- Style
- Legibility
- Neatness

The grade analysis form shown below serves two purposes. It will help the teacher to critically and consistently evaluate a major project as objectively as possible. And attaching a copy of the completed form to the project will show the student in detail the reasons for the grade given for the project.

GRADE ANALYSIS FORM—RESEARCH PROJECT			
	Very Good	Fair	Poor
1. Organization of material			
2. Accuracy in following directions for the assignment			
3. Emphasis on important points			
4. Content			
a. development			
b. clarity			
c. precision			
d. ease of comprehension			
5. Originality of presentation			
6. Creativity			
7. Grammar			
8. Spelling			
9. Completed on time			
10. Neatness			

A format that can be used when grading an oral presentation is shown below. It is important to distribute this form when the assignment is explained, so that the student is aware of what will be considered when an oral presentation is graded. It should also be returned to the student after the presentation is given and evaluated.

GRADE ANALYSIS FORM—ORAL PRESENTATION			
	Very Good	Fair	Poor
1. You were well organized.			
2. You made the important points clear.			
3. You understood the material			
4. You covered the assignment.			
5. You kept the interest of the class.			
6. You were relaxed.			
7. You spoke clearly and loudly.			
8. You had good eye contact.			
9. Your delivery was not too fast.			
10. Your appearance was neat.			
11. You included visuals.			
12. You used notes but did not read your report word for word.			

Final Grade

In addition to considering the grades earned on daily assignments, class discussions, tests, and major projects, you should also consider the following areas when grading a student for the whole semester.

Behavior

1. with other students
2. with the teacher
3. with a substitute teacher
4. with a guest speaker
5. during an assembly
6. during a fire drill
7. during individual work
8. in groupwork

Skill

1. in following directions
2. in listening
3. in thinking
4. in communications
5. in reading
6. in writing
7. in speaking
8. in using resource materials

Attitude

1. toward themselves
2. toward others
3. toward schoolwork
4. toward school property

Knowledge

1. of facts
2. of concepts
3. of processes

Performance

Is the student working up to maximum potential?

Field Trips

Field trips and guest speakers provide a stimulating and worthwhile addition to the curriculum. These activities offer students new educational experiences and encourage community involvement.

This section offers a procedure that could be followed when arranging a field trip or inviting a guest speaker.

Well-planned field trips enrich any curriculum because they give students a more realistic view of the world and an opportunity to explore something beyond their normal everyday experiences. However, it is imperative that field trips be well organized, or chaos will result. Below is a procedure that you should consider using.

1. Decide where you will be going.
2. Get administrative approval.

3. Contact someone at the place where you are going and make arrangements for
   - date of the trip
   - time of the trip
   - number of students expected
   - what the trip will include
   - a guide, if necessary
   - dress requirements, if any
   - lunch, if it is a daylong trip
   - a contact person once you arrive

4. If you are taking the entire class, decide on your form of transportation—parents' cars, bus, or walking—then make the appropriate arrangements.

5. If you are taking from twenty to thirty students on a field trip, it is a good idea to take along another adult for safety purposes.

6. Arrange for permission slips. Each student going on a field trip *must* have a signed parental approval form.

SAMPLE PERMISSION SLIP

My son or daughter, _____, has my permission to go on a field trip to _____ on _____ from 1 P.M.—3 P.M. He or she will be going by bus with approximately thirty other students. The child will be chaperoned by one teacher and one counselor.

Date_____
Parent's Signature _____

If you have any questions please contact me at _____.

Sincerely,

Joan Brown

7. Make arrangements for those students who fail to bring in their permission slips. Ask another teacher to watch these students while you're on the field trip. Make sure these students have a written assignment that will last through the entire class period.

8. Inform your staff members of the field trip. Place a notice in each mailbox stating when the field trip is to take place and which students are going.

9. *Always* keep the administration informed about your plans.

10. The day before the field trip, discuss field-trip behavior with your students. Talk about what will be expected of them on the field trip, what they need to bring, where you will meet, and at what time. Also inform your students what consequences await them if they misbehave on the field trip.

11. Write a thank-you note.

SAMPLE THANK-YOU NOTE

March 2, 1980

Mr. Rupert Brown
Community Relations Officer
United Steel Company
Murray Hill, New Jersey 07974

Dear Mr. Brown:

    Thank you for arranging our visit to the steel plant. Although all of us are constantly using articles made of steel, few of us had any idea of how it is produced. The half day we spent at the United Steel plant was very enlightening for us. The rolling mills and the blast furnace were fascinating.

Sincerely,

Mrs. Emily Ward
Morris Academy

Guest Speakers

A guest speaker can provide a relevant experience for any learning situation. Guest speakers can share with students valuable knowledge from their own experiences. Below is a procedure that could be used in preparing for a guest speaker.

1. Contact the business concern or the person you wish to invite to your classroom, after you have received administrative approval. Arrange a date and a time for the actual visit.
2. Give your speaker an outline, spoken or written, of exactly what you would like covered during the presentation, and specify the allotted time to cover the material.
3. Prepare students for the speaker. Have them think up a list of questions they could ask the speaker. This could be done in groupwork or in a class discussion. Also discuss behavior toward a guest speaker.
4. Have a few students act as a welcoming committee the day the speaker comes. Students should take the speaker's coat, offer coffee (if appropriate), and introduce him or her to the class.
5. If you are planning to videotape the speaker, ask for the speaker's permission, make sure your equipment is set up and working prior to the speaker's arrival.
6. Have a student, or a group of students, write a thank-you note to the speaker.

It is important that students be given time and direction in formulating their own questions for guest speakers so that they are prepared for their visitor. This listing is a sample of the kinds of questions that students would probably want to ask a speaker coming into a Career Exploration class.

1. What exactly do you do for a living?
2. How much education is necessary for your occupational position?
3. How did you get your job?
4. Were there any special requirements for getting your job?
5. Do you think you are receiving adequate pay for the type of work you do? Why or why not?

6. How many hours do you work a week?
7. What type of personality do you need for your work?
8. Do you need further education to maintain your job?
9. Do you have to belong to a union?
10. What is the future job outlook for this career area?
11. Are there many people employed in your line of work?
12. Is there potential for advancement in your occupational field?
13. What are the advantages of your job?
14. What are the disadvantages of your job?
15. What made you choose your career area?

This is an example of the kind of thank-you note you might send to a guest speaker. It should be revised to fit your needs.

January 25, 1980

Miss Margaret Newberger
Jersey News
Madison, New Jersey 07940

Dear Miss Newberger:

Thank you for visiting our Career Awareness class last Thursday. We appreciated your sharing your experiences with us.

Newspaper reporting is a career many of my students are interested in. Thank you for opening our eyes to the long hours, the meticulous research, and the endless editing and rewriting of articles that are also involved. But we also remember what you told us about the joy and satisfaction of seeing your story in print.

We appreciate your taking the time to visit us.

Sincerely,

Mrs. Emily Ward
Morris Academy

3

*The Teacher
and the Students*

THIS SECTION OFFERS AN ASSORTMENT OF IDEAS about how you can knowingly and perceptively develop into a fair, consistent teacher. The sections on Discipline and Promoting a Good Attitude discuss how you can promote a professional relationship with your students. Setting Up Classroom Procedure, Setting Up Groupwork, and Preparing Students for the Instructional Media Center illustrate methods you can use for setting up an effective classroom routine. Reading and the Classroom Teacher, and The Daily Process of Individualization both demonstrate strategies that can be used to meet the varied abilities of your students within a heterogeneous setting.

Promoting a Good Attitude

It is imperative to encourage a good attitude within your classroom setting. If students and teachers understand the rights and responsibilities of their differing roles, an atmosphere conducive to learning and teaching will result. Below are some hints that you may wish to use when working toward developing a healthy classroom attitude.

1. Greet your students each day. If you are outside your door before every class, you can say hello to each student.

2. Put your lesson plans on the chalkboard each day so that students can see what's happening. This is an added security for your slower students.

3. Always write large and legibly on the chalkboard so that everybody can read it easily.

4. Let students know your classroom rules and what the consequences will be should they break one of them. If students know where they stand, fewer misunderstandings will occur.

5. Reserve a few minutes at the beginning of each class for attendance and at the end for cleaning up. This avoids calling desperately for materials when the bell rings.

6. At the end of each class period collect the scissors, books, rulers, glue, pencils, and other things that have been used. Keep track of your materials to use with other classes.

7. Always have your students straighten up a classroom they have used, before leaving it. This will teach them to respect property.

8. Vary your lesson plans. Don't put your students to sleep. Students know when teachers care.

9. If you need audiovisual equipment for a lesson, get it before your class begins. Students should not have to wait while you prepare for class.

10. Try to present your material enthusiastically. Share your knowledge and abilities with your students.

11. Be flexible. Be able to change your plans as necessary. Adjust to fire drills, assemblies, and other interruptions.

12. Overplan so that you can pick and choose activities according to the mood of your class. Be perceptive.

13. Repeat and review your material constantly to make sure your students are grasping the knowledge you are presenting.

14. Evaluate your lesson at the end of each class. If you are teaching the same lesson the next period, consider ways to improve it.

15. Speak loudly and clearly. Make sure the students in the back of the room can hear you.

16. Use words your students can understand, but don't talk down to them.

17. Require silence before giving directions. Don't attempt to scream over student noise. Also, listen attentively to students when they talk to you.

18. Require politeness when students are answering questions or giving opinions in a classroom discussion.

19. Make sure your students answer your questions—not you! Wait for their responses. Don't monopolize a discussion.

20. Help your students and encourage them, but don't do their work for them.

21. Grade your students' papers quickly and return them. Students have a right to know where they stand academically.

22. Be able to admit you are wrong and be able to apologize to a student or a class if the occasion arises.

23. Take time to laugh at a joke with your students.

24. Smile at your students.

25. Praise your students whenever they deserve it.

Setting Up Classroom Procedure

At the beginning of each new semester, introduce yourself, give a brief synopsis of the course you are teaching, discuss your procedures, and explain your classroom rules.

Below is a sample format that was used on the first day in an American Minorities class. This handout was given to each student.

AMERICAN MINORITIES
Goals

1. To explore values and attitudes

2. To examine contributions of various ethnic groups

3. To analyze prejudices and discrimination practices

Units of Study

1. Attitudes

2. The American Indian

3. The American Woman

4. The Immigrant

5. The Afro-American

6. Religious Minorities

Requirements and Grading System

1. Daily assignments must be handed in on time. They are worth one third of your grade.

2. Tests are worth one third of your grade.

3. You will have one major assignment for each ten-week period. These assignments will be worth one third of your grade.

Classroom Procedure

1. Be punctual. If you are late without an excuse, you will be expected to remain 15 minutes after school.

2. Your work must be handed in on time. No late papers will be accepted unless there is a really good reason.

3. Bring a pencil and your work to class every day. This is your responsibility.

4. Please respect and cooperate with your classmates and with me. We will be involved in groupwork, in individual assignments, and in many discussions. Remember, every one deserves the right to learn.

5. Please respect all classroom property.

6. Remember, you are here to succeed, and I am here to help you succeed!

7. You are expected to maintain normal classroom discipline at all times. Follow the instructions of your teacher for fire drills, assemblies, or other special situations.

This handout should be read aloud and explained to each new class. Answer students' questions patiently and in detail. In this manner many misunderstandings may be avoided.

The first day and the first week of a new semester are of utmost importance because it is at this time that the attitude and the routine is set up for the entire semester.

Setting Up Groupwork

Groupwork is a teaching method that encourages student cooperation, the sharing of ideas and talents, and creativity. Below are some suggestions you might use when adapting this technique to fit your particular classroom needs.

1. Prepare a handout direction sheet. Give each student a copy. Explain the assignment in detail. Tell students to make notes on their copy. Answer their questions about the project.

2. Explain to students the criteria you will use to grade them.

3. Explain to students the type of behavior you expect from them in a groupwork situation. Explain that the groups will be disbanded if members do not conduct themselves properly.

4. Show students where the resource materials will be kept during the duration of the project. Demonstrate how one uses a reference book correctly.

5. Make students aware of posters, charts, pictures, maps, and so forth, that have been displayed on the bulletin board.

6. Show students where the art supplies and paper will be kept during this project.

7. Explain to students how you want the room arranged during groupwork.

8. Have students pick their own groupwork partner or partners. Groups of two or three students seem to work out best. However, if you happen to have a student who desires to work alone, allow that possibility.

9. After roll is taken, have the students arrange the desks for groupwork.

10. Allow students 5 minutes before the end of each class to collect materials and to straighten up the room.

11. Walk around the room several times during the hour to see if students need your help. Let the students know you are available to give assistance.

12. Glance through students' papers every other day to see how they are getting along. Some groups will need your help, others your encouragement.

Using the Instructional Media Center

The Instructional Media Center (IMC) offers a wide range of educational resources for the students' use. By using this facility, students are given a chance to acquire skills in locating information, researching, and using the audiovisual equipment. Therefore students should be properly instructed on how to use this center. Below is a procedure that will help your students make use of the IMC.

1. Inform students of the seating arrangement that will be used when the class is in the school library.

2. Discuss the type of behavior you expect in the IMC. Inform students what the consequences will be if they misbehave.

3. Make sure students understand what the assignment is before you take your class to the IMC.

4. If you are taking paper and art supplies to the IMC, tell students where these materials are to be placed.

5. Place a note on the outside of your classroom door, stating where your class is. Someone may need to contact you or one of your students.

6. The first trip you make to the IMC with your class should begin with a lecture by either you or the librarian. Students must be taught how to find and how to use resource materials. Students should be shown how to use the card catalog, the *Readers' Guide,* atlases, reference books, and audiovisual materials. Also familiarize them with the physical layout of the IMC.

7. Inform students that they must replace the materials they use and straighten up the area before leaving.

The Daily Process of Individualization

Every student is an individual with specific abilities and needs. Classroom teachers must be prepared to offer their pupils individualized experiences. This can be done on a daily basis in a traditional classroom setting as well as in an open classroom situation. Below are several suggestions.

- If most of your materials are read aloud, your slower students will at least hear the material.

- Quietly adjust the difficulty (or scope) of daily assignments to fit the capabilities of your slower students so they can cover the same material but with an assignment they can do.

- Arrange for your slower students to take their tests orally whenever possible. Students who have a difficult time communicating their thoughts in writing may be able to communicate better orally.

- When doing groupwork encourage your slower students to pair up with better students. By doing this, your slower students will be able to verbalize thoughts that a better student can record in written form.

- Arrange an extra-credit file so that all your students will have something interesting and worthwhile to do in their spare time.

- Have special projects set aside for those students who have the desire and talent to do them. Encourage academic curiosity.

- Ask your students often if they need help. Walk around your classroom frequently and encourage your students to do their best.

- Make sure everyone understands your directions, even if you have to repeat them five times in five different ways.

- Compliment your students as a class and as individuals.

- Let your slower students answer the less difficult questions in a discussion.

- Let your brighter students answer the more difficult questions.

- Place your activity directions on the chalkboard each day so that students can refer to them if they wish.

- If possible, arrange for student helpers to tutor your slower students.

- Use words that all your students will understand.

- Constantly review your material, even if it is for 5 minutes every other day.

Reading and the Classroom Teacher

It is not unusual to encounter a high percentage of students who are unable to read the required textbooks. This may occur because the textbooks were poorly selected or because the students are reading way below their grade level.

Since this is so, it becomes the teacher's responsibility to present the textbook to the students in a way that is understandable. A teacher can accomplish this by using the method suggested. This particular technique familiarizes the students with their reading material and helps to meet the needs of the slower students.

1. Introduce the entire book to the class. Go through the Table of Contents and give a short explanation of each chapter.

2. If there are charts or a glossary in the back of the book, make students aware of this. Show how to use these reading aids.

3. Point out where the index is. Explain how to use it.

4. When introducing a new chapter make sure new vocabulary words and new concepts are introduced by way of a dictionary assignment or a lecture.

5. Read the material aloud. This way the students will see and hear the material simultaneously. Remember, call on those students who volunteer to read. Don't embarrass students who can't read by asking them to read aloud.

6. Continually ask students to summarize the material being read to see if they are grasping the main concepts.

7. Point out all maps, charts, and pictures that are included within the chapter and comment on each.

8. Encourage students to use context clues when attempting to grasp an idea or a concept.

Discipline

There will be fewer discipline problems and fewer discipline referrals if the teacher keeps the following points in mind.

1. Set up a classroom procedure and routine so that students will know what to do and exactly what is expected of them. This gives students a sense of security. They know exactly where they stand.

2. Be consistent and firm with your students at all times. Set up your rules and adhere to them. For example, if three unexcused tardies means 15 minutes after school, then keep track of the tardies and follow up on them.

3. Let students know what consequences will follow what actions. This should be discussed on the first day of class. For example, insubordination may result in a three-day suspension.

4. Respect your students as people.

5. Don't be afraid to let your students know that you care for them and that you are proud of them. If they know you feel that way they'll rarely let you down.

6. Take the time to smile and to greet your students at the beginning of each class.

7. Show that you have a sense of humor—laugh once in a while.

8. Dress neatly and act professionally. Dress and act like an adult and a teacher.

9. Keep your classroom neat and have each class clean up after themselves. Sometimes if a classroom looks orderly, your students will act orderly.

10. Be prepared, be organized, be enthusiastic, be helpful, and be courteous.

11. Make sure your assignments are realistic. Do your students understand the assignment? Do they have enough knowledge to do the assigned work? Do they have enough time to accomplish the work you expect of them without being rushed?

12. Don't overwork your students or they will become resentful and eventually cause trouble. Change your tactics once in a while. Read a play together or play a game.

13. Give students at least a week's notice before a test so that they can study and be prepared. Give them a chance to pass.

14. Get help if you need it. Administrators, counselors, and parents may be more effective than you in certain situations.

15. Don't argue with a student in front of the class. Take the student out in the hall and discuss the problem there or wait until after class. Don't resort to unprofessional methods.

16. Don't raise your voice all the time. Sometimes it is more effective to remain quiet or to speak very quietly.

17. Do not insult a student verbally or physically.

18. Sometimes it is best to overlook a situation. If you corrected everything, you would waste time and become ineffective. Remember, students are human and they do make mistakes.

19. Be fair to all your students. Do not discriminate against a student. Be careful of favoritism.

20. Don't make idle threats. Do what you say you will do.

4

The Teacher
as a Professional

Teachers are accountable for their own actions and have a responsibility to act professionally in their dealings with students, with colleagues, and with administrators. They also have to remain intellectually attuned to the current developments in their area of specialization. Discussions on professional behavior and growth are contained in this chapter.

Professional Behavior

The sampling below offers a few guidelines that teachers may wish to consider when interacting within their school environment.

- Teachers should dress, act, and speak appropriately in the classroom. Students resent teachers who try to look, act, and talk like students. You have something to offer your student as an adult, and you should feel comfortable within this situation.

- Treat administrators, teaching colleagues, parents, and students with respect and you will be respected. This does not imply that you cannot disagree with any of these groups. It just means that there are tactful and productive ways of handling situations.

- Always treat the school secretaries and custodians with a great deal of respect and consideration. Remember these people are part of the entire professional team that runs the school.

- Never discuss a student's problem in front of other students or in random conversation with other teachers. This is a breach of confidence.

- Never repeat anything a colleague tells you in confidence.

- You are paid to teach the slow, the average, and the gifted student. All students should be taught. Students resent teachers who say, "The assignment is on the board, get to work," or those who do nothing but joke around.

- Always remain in control and act responsibly. You are the teacher and you owe your students an education.

- Never strike a student or swear at one. This is unprofessional behavior. Never ridicule a student. Resolve the problem in the hall, or send the student to the office. Ridiculing may make you feel great for a moment, but in the long run you might lose the respect of your other students.

- Teachers do have deadlines to meet. Always hand in your attendance records, locker lists, fourth-Friday counts, order forms, and grades on time.

- Teachers should act in a respectable and professional manner during parent-teacher conferences. Teachers should be honest, helpful, and tactful when discussing a student's academic and citizenship status with the student's parents.

The Teacher and the Administration

Because a teacher is part of the bureaucratic organization, it is necessary to keep the administration informed. With good communication, you should receive support for any project that is planned and backing for any major discipline problem that might arise. Some sample situations that could demand administrative support are listed below.

1. Get approval for any field trip you plan.

2. Get clearance for any guest speaker you wish to invite into your classroom.

3. If you are a sponsor for any student club or student activity, keep the administration informed about your plans.

4. Get permission to go to any conference you wish to attend.

5. Ask for administrative support in handling the really difficult discipline problems.

6. If medical attention is needed for a student, inform the administration immediately.

7. If you suspect a child is being abused at home, it is your legal responsibility to inform the administration immediately.

8. If you are doing an unusual unit or lesson with a class, invite an administrator in and share it. Share the good as well as the bad.

9. Compliment and thank your administrators when they deserve it.

Professional Growth

As a professional, one should continue to grow intellectually and academically. Be prepared to spend some time and money on this ongoing process. Listed below are a few suggestions that will aid you in your professional growth.

- Take an occasional graduate class at a university or begin working on your master's degree. Know what's going on in your field. Take classes and stay stimulated.

- Attend workshops and conferences. Find out what other districts are doing. See what new textbooks are available.

- Join the national council or the state association for your subject area and attend their conferences.

- Subscribe to educational journals and keep abreast of new educational trends.

- Continually preview new materials within your field. Write to publishers and ask for complimentary materials.

- Subscribe to and read a few current-events magazines regularly. Keep in touch with what is going on in the world and incorporate this knowledge into your lesson plans.

- Maintain an adequate library of books related to your field. Have reference books available to answer to any questions.

- Be willing to share ideas with your peers. Trade materials and ideas. Adapt ideas to fit your classroom needs.

5

The First-Year Teacher

A FIRST-YEAR TEACHER OFTEN FACES A SITUATION very different from the one encountered in student teaching. For the first time one is totally responsible for the students within a specific classroom situation.

There is a commonality in the types of problems all inexperienced teachers face when new at the job, and students will insist on testing a new teacher. This section focuses on the most common problems that may be encountered in the first year.

Very often new teachers go home at night wondering if they'll ever make it and if they chose the wrong profession. This is not an unusual concern. The following suggestions should be considered if you are a beginning teacher.

1. Students will test you. They want to see how far they can push you. They want to find out if you're easy or hard. The best bet is to be firm. When you say no, mean it. Your tone of voice is important.

2. It is easy to assume authority on the outside. However, students will sometimes react negatively when you demand something. They will make you feel unreasonable, even though you know you are right and your decision is a good one. Sometimes a student's reaction will hurt you. This type of reaction will go away in time. After all, you are new at this—the responsibility, the hassles, and the disciplining.

3. Grading sometimes causes anxiety because most teachers are concerned with whether or not they are being fair. You will find a happy medium in this area. Just make sure your students understand from the beginning exactly what it is that you require. If you have to, read aloud examples of an *A, B,* and *C* paper so they get the idea. Also, correct, grade, and pass papers back as soon as possible. Halfway through each marking period, let your students know how they are doing and how they can improve.

4. Learn to space your assignments so that you do not end up with twenty-five sets of papers to grade at once. Remember, students are capable of grading certain papers as a group in class.

5. Sometimes beginning teachers have difficulty timing a lesson. The best thing to do in this case is to overplan, then you'll never run short.

6. Learn to be flexible. Sometimes your lesson plans do not go as planned. For example, if your students are involved in an excellent discussion, let it continue. Or maybe a new magazine has just arrived with a great play in it. Read it in class and discuss it. Permit yourself to be academically spontaneous.

7. First-year teachers are often afraid to attempt new teaching methods because they lack confidence. Just remember, the first time is the most difficult. The second time is easier and more enjoyable.

8. Don't be afraid to fail. Try things, and if they work be happy. If they don't, either toss the idea aside or rework it. Be able to evaluate yourself, your ideas, and your presentations fairly and honestly.

9. If you don't know the answer to a question, don't bluff. Just admit that you do not know the answer, and state that you will attempt to find out what it is.

10. Make sure your students understand you. Use a vocabulary they can relate to. When you introduce a new word, make sure you explain what it means.

11. Discipline can be a touchy area for the first-year teacher. Remember you owe your entire class the right to learn. Students who disrupt that right need to be disciplined. A telephone call to a parent, a note to the student's counselor, a discipline referral, a student-teacher meeting, or keeping the student after school are all things to consider when disciplining becomes necessary.

12. Be consistent and save yourself at least twenty-five discipline referrals. Set up classroom rules and classroom procedures from Day One. Then the students will know exactly where they stand.

13. Learn to relax and enjoy your classes. This can be done in a professional manner. It is possible to have a pleasant conversation with students without becoming their best friend. Maintain your distance, or you will have discipline problems resulting from familiarity.

14. Get to know your staff members. Learn from them and have fun with them.

15. Don't make teaching your entire life. Have outside friends who are not teachers. Develop hobbies, travel, watch TV, read mysteries, write books, do anything—but give yourself a break!

6

The Student Teacher

THE STUDENT TEACHER ARRIVES WITH THEORETICAL knowledge, but without the tested procedures, planning, and experiences that come with actual classroom interaction. Therefore it is your responsibility to provide, during this apprenticeship period, the direction, the training, and the atmosphere through which the necessary skills and understanding can be developed.

It is the responsibility of the critic teacher to demand the highest level of professionalism from the student teacher. This is difficult and time consuming, but not impossible.

Included in this section are ideas on how to encourage a student teacher in professional development. A suggested checklist, to be used by the critic teacher when grading a student teacher, is also included.

You and Your Student Teacher

The following information should be considered by the critic teacher to ensure a professional environment in which a student teacher can learn and develop.

1. In the beginning of the critic teacher-student teacher relationship, give your student teacher an explanation of

   - your teaching philosophy
   - your teaching techniques
   - your classroom procedures
   - your department's course offerings
   - what is currently being taught in your classroom
   - what you expect of a student teacher

2. Give your student teacher a format to follow for lesson plans. Explain when you expect the plans every week. It is advisable to write the first set of plans with your student teacher so that it is clear exactly what you expect in this area.

3. Share your materials—textbooks, reference books, filmstrips, maps, and so forth.

4. Share your teaching ideas occasionally. Do not do this all the time lest you stifle the creativity and initiative of the student teacher.

5. Share your discipline techniques, but give your student teacher the freedom to try different ones.

6. Encourage your student teacher to grow, to be independent, and to try new ideas and methods.

7. Meet with your student teacher at least once a week to discuss your observations and any problems that he or she might be having. Evaluate openly, fairly, and honestly.

8. If you are having a problem with your student teacher, discuss it only with your student teacher and his or her supervisor. Do not discuss it randomly with other staff members.

9. Introduce your student teacher to your staff members individually.

10. Take your student teacher on a tour of your building. Point out where the gym, cafeteria, restrooms, teachers' lounge, and auditorium are located.

11. Encourage your student teacher to visit other classrooms, so that he or she is exposed to teaching methods other than your own.

Checklist

The following checklist could be very helpful in directing a student teacher. The student teacher who is aware of your expectations will do a better job.

1. Attendance and attitude

_____ Reports on time

_____ Calls if late

_____ Calls if absent

_____ Leaves at correct time

_____ Knows the physical layout of the building

_____ Knows fellow staff members and utilizes their talents

_____ Good attendance record

2. Classroom observation

_____ Objective of the lesson being taught

_____ Materials being used

_____ Knowledge of subject matter being taught

_____ Student activities

_____ Teaching methods

_____ Evaluation methods

_____ Student-teacher relationship

_____ Classroom organization

_____ Classroom management

_____ Classroom discipline

_____ Physical factors of the classroom

3. Lesson plans

_____ Completed on time

_____ Follow a specific format

_____ Are varied

_____ Are innovative

_____ Are organized

_____ Are detailed

_____ Are well presented

_____ Are left in case of absence

4. Assumption of teacher duties and responsibilities

_____ Takes roll

_____ Assigns seats

_____ Keeps students' records

_____ Knows students' names

_____ Checks papers

_____ Prepares bulletin boards

_____ Prepares materials (handouts)

_____ Previews materials (books, filmstrips)

_____ Keeps room in order

_____ Keeps track of materials (books, rulers)

_____ Gets help for students when they need it

_____ Maintains discipline

_____ Engages in after-school activities

_____ Attends staff meetings

_____ Knows what to do in case of an emergency

_____ Is well prepared

_____ Is on time for class

5. Personal evaluation

_____ Is professional

_____ Is pleasant

_____ Is competent

_____ Treats students with respect

_____ Dresses appropriately

_____ Accepts constructive criticism

_____ Treats staff members with respect

6. Relationship with critic teacher

_____ Asks for suggestions

_____ Evaluates plans

_____ Has weekly conferences

_____ Follows regular classroom procedure

_____ Asks for assistance

_____ Encourages the student teacher

_____ Helps in planning lessons

_____ Evaluates lesson plans

_____ Works with the student teacher's college supervisor

_____ Grades fairly and honestly

Epilogue

AFTER READING THIS GUIDE YOU WILL HAVE A better understanding of the various qualities and skills needed to function efficiently and productively as a teacher. Many of the procedures and methods that have been suggested should be of help to both the veteran and the inexperienced teacher. Some of the ideas presented should help an experienced teacher to revitalize an existing program. For the new teacher, these suggestions should make teaching easier, less time consuming, and more rewarding. Ideally, *Hints for Classroom Teachers* will serve as a reference manual for student teachers, as a daily guide for new teachers, and as a stimulating resource for veteran teachers.

1 2 3 4 5 6 7 8 9 10—PP—85 84 83 82 81 80 79